...how we recreated the pioneering movies of the Lumiere Brothers

...how students rediscovered the lost art of the magic lantern

... and how Pepper's Ghost returned to Regent Street!

Foreword

This is book is indeed an 'extravaganza'. In a very small space, it manages to bring together the histories of photography, animation and film along with reminders of the places and moments where this history unfolded. I was honoured to be a very small part of the celebration of this story and of the students' work so I'm very glad to be here inside the front cover too!

We might ask why the history of photography and cinematography is so little known? Is it because these are art forms that appear to be fleeting? We look or watch and then get up and go? Perhaps that's the case for cinema yet photography has become the art form of everyone's living room walls and mantlepieces, though perhaps people are inclined to think of the photos as 'true' representations of their relatives rather than artistic ones.

In fact, the histories covered by this book are fascinating while some are hidden in plain sight. Just one example: I've known of the old Polytechnic building in Regents Street, all my life. My father studied there in the 1930s and I've walked past it every time I've worked for BBC Radio over the last 50 years. Did I know of the extraordinary part the Polytechnic building has played in the stories told in this book? Absolutely not!

I hope you will be equally surprised and delighted by what you find here and that you revel in what it reveals about these great creative industries.

Professor Michael Rosen

Professor Pepper's
OPTICAL
Extravaganza

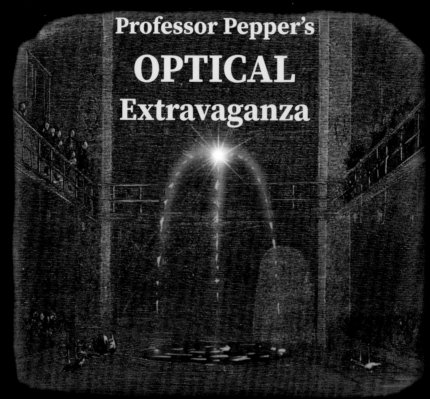

in 1854 an illuminated cascade fascinated visitors to the Royal Polytechnic.

by
Henry Pepper FCS, (A.INST) CE
Principal Lecturer and Director, Royal Polytechnic Institution
and
Stephen Ryley MA (RCA) SFHEA
Principal Lecturer, BA Animation, University of Westminster

Publishers: Independent Publishing Network, for The University of Westminster,   309 Regent Street,   London
First Edition   First Published 2022   ©   Printed in England, surprisingly.

The University of Westminster's antecedent organisation was the world's first Polytechnic, and opened at 309 Regent Street in 1838.

THE ROYAL POLYTECHNIC INSTITUTION,

INCORPORATED BY ROYAL CHARTER, A.D. 1838,

FOR THE ADVANCEMENT OF

THE ARTS AND PRACTICAL SCIENCE;

Image Courtesy of University of Westminster Archives

The Great Hall of the Polytechnic was a place of
"abominable smells and the odd explosion"
as demonstrations of the latest technologies,
including the diving bell, were made to the public.
Can you spot the figure on the trapeze? He was an automaton.

...ne diving pool,
...one shilling you
...end in the diving

...threw pennies
...pool, which the
...diver would then

...bert paid a visit,
...in the diving bell,
...t so much that he
...he patron.

...modelled his
...uth Kensington
...Museum on our
...c.

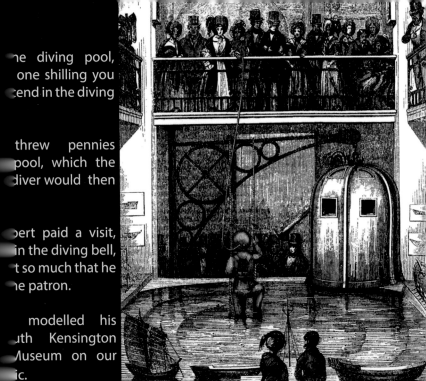

Interior of the Diving-Bell, at the Polytechnic, Regent Street.

...low the door knocker says
...ck once for more air"

Anxious-looking Aquanauts would
enter and exit the diving bell
through this square hole in the floor.

INTERIOR OF THE POLYTECHNIC INSTITUTION, SHOWING THE DIVING BELL.

The Great Hall: in 1831, and in 2016

Even though the Great Hall has now been sliced into sections,
the ceiling remains unchanged.

The Polytechnic was one of the very first institutions to demonstrate the new invention of photography, and in 1841, Europe's first commercial portrait photography studio opened on the roof.

It featured a specially constructed glass pyramid, to let in lots of daylight.

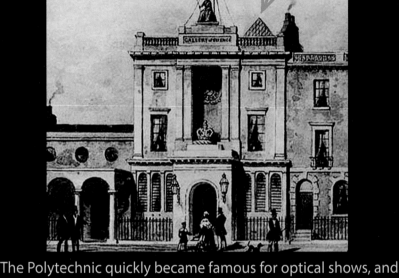

The Polytechnic quickly became famous for optical shows, and so a purpose-built projection theatre was added. This is now our Regent Street Cinema, which is the world's oldest working cinema, and a cherished part of the University of Westminster.

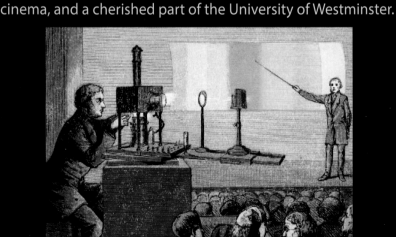

One satisfied customer wrote a review of his visit to the
Polytechnic:

"The Institution in Regent Street,
where an infinite variety of ingenious models
are exhibited and explained,
and where lectures comprising a quantity of information
on many practical subjects are delivered,
is a great public benefit and a wonderful place".

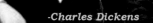

-*Charles Dickens*

A 26-year-old chemist called Henry Pepper was hired to give
lectures, and within 6 years he had become the principal
lecturer and director of the Poly.
Pepper developed the optical theatre, and demonstrated stage
illusions, including his latest invention "Pepper's Ghost", a trick
still in use today (we now call it a stage hologram)

Pepper first used his ghost illusion to create the special effects
for a Christmas Ghost story by (you guessed it) Charles Dickens.

Our Prof then set up evening classes, allowing busy Londoners
greater access to further education.

Here we see Professor Pepper
demonstrating cutting-edge
technology.
This gigantic induction coil
contained 3 miles of wire and was
able to create a lightning bolt
over one metre long.

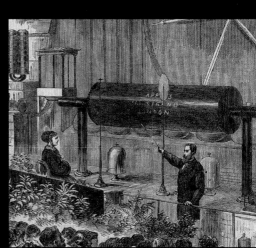

Around the 1880s we enjoyed a period of rapid growth, and even today our students still benefit from the legacy of philanthropist Quintin Hogg, who took over the Polytechnic.

If you are a fan of educational field trips, you will be pleased to learn that we offered the world's first package holidays.
The Polytechnic teamed up with Sir Henry Lunn to form a travel company called "Lunn-Poly", which is now rebranded as *Tui*.

Our famous projection theatre became Britain's first cinema, when the Lumiere Brothers premiered their brand new "Cinematographe" in 1896.
We still use the cinema, and our graduation films are shown there every year.

We love sports!
In 1908 we organised the opening ceremony of the Olympic Games, and were also responsible for setting up the first modern marathon.

By the 1970s we were offering the first ever degree courses in Photographic Science, Photography and Media Studies.

In 1992 we became the University of Westminster, and in 2001 we launched London's first BA in Animation, which runs alongside our Film and Television production courses.

Animation graduate
Yousif Al-Khalifa

Animation

Animation was exhibited and demonstrated at 309 Regent Street from day one.

Before photography, film or television were even conceived, the balcony of the Great Hall featured two large spinning discs, called 'Phenakistascopes'.

By peering through the slots, figures and objects would magically spring to life.

Professor Pepper wrote about these wonders, and even gave a short masterclass in animation production:

"At the Polytechnic Institution there are two of these wheels, with looking -glasses, and although the same designs have done duty for many years, they still attract the public attention."

"This is a most amusing instrument; it consists of a disc made of stout cardboard, upon which, towards the edge, a series of figures in eight or ten different positions is painted. Thus if it is wished to produce the illusion of a man running, the first position should be quiescent, standing upright, the second advancing forward a little, the third stepping out still more, and so on to the sixth figure, which should be drawn as if running at full speed; the remaining attitudes should show the person gradually returning to the first quiet attitude."

The Return of Professor Pepper

Our first project was an animated timeline, charting the history of optics, from the pinhole to the pixel.

We needed a narrator to play the part of Professor Pepper, and Michael Rosen kindly agreed to help.

Once the sound tracks were recorded, our animation students set to work, producing 15 films, each presenting an important moment in the history of optics.
You can see them on our blogsite:
https://lumiere125.wordpress.com/

1: Meet the Professor
by Kian Ali & Hana Bhatti
An introduction to the history of optics, from the pixel to the pinhole, presented by Professor Henry Pepper from the Royal Polytechnic Institution

2: Butades' Daughter
by Aimee Langford & Emily Wloch
People have been making silhouette images since the dawn of humanity; they are our first attempts to capture an image.

3: Al Hazan's Artificial Eye
by Reece Anderson-Watson & Arif Ullah
The amazing projecting properties of pinholes.

4: Seneca's Lentil
by Zarin Sarwar & Scott Formosa
The word 'lens' comes from lentil, as they have a similar shape. Adding a lens is a real game changer, as we will see.

5: Fantastic Phantasms
by Haran Arulselvam & Arsalan Malik
A projector is just a camera, turned inside-out. People were getting up to mischief with them from the very start.

6: Watch the Birdie
by Rachel Lewis
The birth of photography, and a battle between two rival formats.

7: Julia's Chicken Shed
by Hannah Miller & Ines Carvalho Portela
One of the first artists to explore the creative potential of photography was Julia Cameron

8: Pepper's Ghost
by Abigail Lindon & Denis Osammor
A stage illusion developed for Dickens, which is still in use today.

9: Wheatstone's Wonder
by Samuel Oware & Bruno Coelho
If you thought virtual reality was a new thing, think again!

10: Time in Motion
by Eleanor King & Katy O'Neill
Eadweard Muybridge was an extremely odd fellow, but years ahead of his time.

11: The Wizard of Menlo Park
by Paul Tabarcia & Cristian Mesa Torres
Thomas Edison, and his many 'lightbulb moments'.

12: Le Cinematographe
by Lauren Birch & El-Mar Cabello
The Lumiere Brothers perfected the movie camera, and screened their first film in 1895

13: Alice's Wonderland
by Melanie Martin & Christina Pop
Alice Guy Blache was the first to realise the potential of narrative films, and became an extremely successful movie director.

14: Birth of the Pixel
by Chouiab Raziq

Logie Baird, the inventor of steampunk mechanical television

15: Glorious Technicolor
by Kevin Egemba & Alan Saavedra

Have you ever wondered what R.G.B. stands for?

The title sequence

The titles for the animated series, and for this book, were created by animation tutor Mateusz Gidaszewski.

The Quintin Hogg Trust

All of the projects described in this book were made possible with the generous support of the Quintin Hogg Trust, who provided funding with the aim of enabling, enhancing and extending the student experience at the University of Westminster.
Quintin himself was a pupil of Professor Pepper, and later took over the running of the Polytechnic.

Gizmos

Our next project was an opportunity for students to become inventors, and recreate some amazing optical wonders, using household items and upcycled packaging materials.

They then made animated films, to demonstrate how to construct them.

Our foundation level art & design students produced the title sequence for these DIY films. This was their first experience of traditional lightbox animation. We edited their "morphs" into loops, illustrating the idea that each invention is part of a constantly evolving chain of discovery and innovation.

1: Camera Obscura
by Alice Siniscalchi & Kerrie Portman

This magic box allows you to draw photo-realistic images!

2: Nipkow Disc
by Milena French, Finn Woodruff & Marvin Ramirez

Pictures made from dots

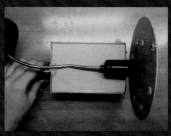

3: Pinhole Solarscope
by Hasah Saeed, Kai Conlon & Adrian Zabala

The safe way to enjoy a solar eclipse.

4: Fox Talbot Camera

by Elena Chasiakou, Rukba Emmarie & Adam Tew

Here's how to take a 'Victorian Polaroid' using a fish bowl and some glow-in-the-dark paper.

5: Pepper's Ghost

by Ana Pereira do Prado Lima & Joao Viera

An old CD case holds the secret to summoning Pepper's Ghost

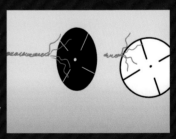

6: Magic Lantern

by Artemis Mitropoulou, Vincas Mikulenas & Ibraheem Elthaferi

All projectors are based on this simple principle.

7: Zoopraxinoscope

by Preslava Lyubenova, Dorottya Seemann & Josie Walshe

Luckily this optical wonder is easier to make, than to say

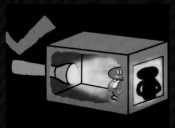

8: Silhouette Maker

by Antigona Dino, Louis Hines & Samuel Knox

Instantly convert any 3D object to 2D

9: RGB Colour Wheel
by Ali Tezgel, Crockett Macnie & Jamal Jadunandan
This gizmo demonstrates how you can get a full colour image from just red green and blue light.

10: stereo scope
by Ottilie Collingridge, Kishan Singh & Samuel Bryant
It is strange to realise that a pair of 2D pictures can make us think we are seeing a 3D object.

... and *the one that got away* !

This group of animation students then went on to design, and start building full-sized contraptions. These were scheduled to be exhibited at the education centre of the Heath Robinson Museum, but sadly, we had to quickly cancel the project half-way through, due to the Covid-19 lockdown.

A full-size silhouette portrait making machine under construction in our 3D workshops by Louis Hines, Antigona Dino & Samuel Knox

Magic Lanterns: Victorian Imax

Inside the Projection Box of the Optical Theatre, c. 1850
On the left, you can see one of the powerful lanterns. Lumps of lime were burnt in an intensely hot flame of hydrogen gas, mixed with oxygen. A risky process which required very careful handling, this brilliant source of illumination, known as "limelight" enabled Pepper's projectors to throw an image onto an enormous screen of 648 square feet.

His large-format lantern slides were unique to the Polytechnic; bigger and better than any that could be seen elsewhere. This was indeed high definition, big-screen entertainment!

Here is Professor Pepper, describing the effect with relish:

"At the Polytechnic sometimes six lanterns are in use at one and the same time; besides a host of accessory apparatus behind the screen for the production of noise. - thunder, wind, cannon shots, the roars of hungry beasts etc, are all imitated with great success.

A plate is appended represeting the efforts to imitiate the horrors of war during the siege of Delhi."

Victorian PowerPoint

Magic Lanterns Return to Regent Street

As part of our celebrations, we staged our own magic lantern show in the cinema. This "Victorian PowerPoint" charted the history of 309 Regent Street, and it's place at the heart of optical science and innovation.

BA Illustration students, Milica Simovic and Mely Montemayor Ayala created our magic lantern slides, which were projected using a working copy of a Riley Brothers Praestantia Machine.

Stephen Ryley on the stage of the Regent Street Cinema

The Royal Institution

The Royal Institution is only 800 metres south of 309 Regent Street.
It opened in 1799, with a similar mission to our own Royal Polytechnic, to *"introduce new technologies and teach science to the general public through lectures and demonstrations"*.

The Royal Institution is famous for its annual Christmas Lectures, which have been running now for nearly 200 years.
Here we see the eminent scientist Michael Faraday delivering a Christmas Lecture in 1855.

Back at the Poly, Professor Pepper also offered his own series of Christmas lectures and other diversions. It appears that Pepper and Faraday were on good terms, because Faraday was given a VIP tour behind the scenes at the Poly, where Pepper revealed the science behind his Ghost illusion.

"Very few persons could understand how the ghost was produced, although many persons wrote about and explained it; even the distinguished philosopher, Michael Faraday, when I took him behind the scenes, said, with his usual love of truth: "Do you know, Mr. Pepper, I really don't understand it." I then took his hand, and put it on one of the huge glass plates, when he said, " Ah ! now I comprehend it; but your glasses are kept so well protected I could not see them even behind your scenes."

Christmas Lectures 2020

We had the opportunity to rekindle this relationship, when our animation students were invited by Windfall Films to create the titles for the 2020 Christmas Lectures.

The challenge: the students were invited to devise a title sequence, capturing ther main themes of the three hour-long programmes, which explored the cyclic nature of the Earth. Topics included the carbon cycle, volcanoes, the ocean currents, whales, and sustainability.

The lectures were titled "Planet Earth: A User's Guide"

"Eat More Chocolate" by Alice Siniscalchi

The production company wanted a textured look for the animation, to match their set. Fortunately, one of the students had developed a very similar style for a film that she had made in the first year of the course, and the clients were happy for us to go ahead in this style.

The problem: we had just 10 days to make the finished animation.
.... and we were all working under lockdown restrictions.

The students quickly pooled their ideas, and developed an 'animatic' which is a rough version of the animation.

The "User's Guide" made us think of the Ikea man, who appears on instructions for flat pack furniture.

the Animatic

The animation team was:

Artemis Mitroupolou, Antigona Dino, Finn Woodruff, Kishan Singh, Kerrie Portman, Milena French, Adam Tew, Preslava Lyubenova, Louis Hines, Vincas Mikulenas, Ana Prada Lima and Alice Siniscalchi.

Ten days later: the Finished Work

The title also appeared in the Faraday Lecture theatre throughout the broadcasts.

photo: Chris Jackson

Windfall's Series Director, Henry Fraser said:

"The title sequence for this year's Christmas Lectures is stunning. It pulls together a huge amount of content from all three lectures in a coherent, dynamic and visually compelling way.
For a subject as big as the Earth this was no mean feat. We are extremely grateful to all the hard working students who contributed to the animation and hope you can all enjoy it on your tv screens on BBC4 over Christmas!"

you can see the lectures at the Royal Institution website:
https://www.rigb.org/explore-science/explore/video/planet-earth-users-guide-air-2020

Christmas Lectures 2021

A new team of students tackled the titles for the 2021 Lectures.
The theme this time was Viruses; how they spread, how we detect them, and how we are fighting back. We developed a James Bond inspired sequence, starring Dr Sarah Gilbert, which we called "*the Girl with the Golden Jab*"

The project was led by a level 5 Animation Student, Charly Korda, who said:
"We had such a large team this year, so it was quite an exciting feat to produce and coordinate this many people. I'm really thankful for the team's quality and adaptability along the way."

The Team: *Nadine Abdelaziz, Nathan Adenaike, Jauhar Asharaf, Babatunde Balogun, Akua Brooks, Ilirian Camaj, Joseph Conway, Jonna Del Rosario, Leonardo Fernandes Davies, Isabella Hernandez Villegas, Elizabeth Judah, Aaisha Khan, Elle Klein, Charly Korda, Aly-Qyzer Ladhu, Maria Moran, Felicity Neal, Stephen Nelson, Aimee Nkansah-Badu, Jessica Ojobor, Chika Okechukwu, Kokila Paramanantham, Hiral Patel, Nada Riaz, Joseph Shepherd, Brigita Tarakanovaite and Kyot Tun.*

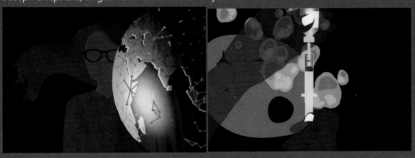

You can see the lectures on the BBC iPlayer
https://www.bbc.co.uk/iplayer/episode/m0012tzd/royal-institution-christmas-lectures-2021-1-the-invisible-enemy

Pioneers of Portrait Photography

The science and art of Photography have occupied pride of place in the history of the University, from the earliest days.

Just one year after the Poly first opened its doors, Louis Daguerre in France, and William Henry Fox Talbot in England each independently launched processes to make a permanent record of images.

Louis' *Daguerrotype* was a tiny, one-off photograph.
However, Henry's *Talbotype* used paper negatives, from which any number of positive prints could be made; the basis of nearly all subsequent photography, right up until the arrival of digital cameras.

The French Government were delighted with Daguerre, and awarded him a generous state pension of 6,000 francs (roughly equivalent to £60,000 per year, today).
This was given on the condition that the French state would then adopt his invention, and generously donate it to the entire world.

This did not deter the wily Frenchman from swiftly arranging a patent covering England, Wales and the Colonies.
This was the only patent he held.

Let us stop and think about this situation for a moment.

Imagine you are in Victorian England, and have just learnt about this amazing new technological marvel, which, for the first time, is capable of accurately and swiftly capturing the likeness of anyone, and recording it permanently.

You discover that the invention is protected by a patent covering your territory. Let us now assume that you are the sort of person who has an entrepreneurial spirit, lots of courage, and a very useful amount of disposable cash.

Conclusion? You could quickly acquire this patent, giving you exclusive rights to the Daguerrotype process, and set yourself up as Britain's first commercial portrait photographer.

You would have a legally enforceable monopoly on the local market, and a quick fortune could be made, surely?

The simple answer is yes..

Oh yes, ...indeedy!

Daguerre eagerly sold his Patent to a London Coal Merchant by the name of Richard Beard, for £800. (which would be about £80,000 today)

Beard set up Europe's very first commercial portrait photography studio, lit with daylight furnished by a specially constructed glass pyramid, on the roof of the Royal Polytechnic Institution building in 1841.

Beard did actually attempt to negotiate a deal with Talbot, to use his process instead.

Why? Well, Talbotypes could be made considerably bigger than Daguerrotypes, and had the obvious commercial advantage that the negatives could produce endless prints

However, the two men could not agree on a deal.
Talbot began to gain a bad reputation for this kind of restrictive control, but to be fair, he had invested a lot of his own money in his invention.

The Polytechnic did manage to negotiate a modest license with Talbot, enabling them to demonstrate his photographic process to a paying audience, and Talbot himself made good use of the optical apparatus that the Polytechnic routinely made available to inventors and engineers.

Being photographed at the Poly swiftly became all the rage amongst fashionable Victorians.
There were separate waiting rooms for the ladies and the gentlemen; of course, who were happy to queue for a considerable time to have their likeness captured using the latest "photogenic drawing" techniques.

Within a few minutes, the sitter was then presented with a tiny Daguerrotype, measuring just 4 x 5 cm, in a smart black presentation case.

Here is a footnote to our story.
It is a detail that you might find deliciously ironic.

When Talbot agreed to have his own portrait taken in our rooftop studio, it was (of course) a **Daguerrotype** that he took home to show his wife.

The Daguerrotype of William Henry Fox Talbot,
taken at 309 Regent Street
by Richard Beard
(shown actual size)

Inside the Studio, 309 Regent Street, 1842
Can you spot the fashionable couple admiring their photos,
through magnifying glasses?

This new experience seemed curious to the wealthy sitters, most of whom were used to chatting and joking casually when having their conventional portraits painted.

In a newspaper article about a visit to the studio published in 1842, Lamann Blanchard joked that

"...here you must sit mute and motionless.
You may wink, you may perhaps put on a smile,
but you must not laugh;
for if you do, one half of your head will go off!"

Beard made a fortune.
Then lost it again (but that is a story for another day)

Photography continued to be a very important part of the Polytechnic's appeal. As the technology improved, and earlier patent restrictions relaxed, the art became much more accessible to a wider, but still well-to-do public.

In 1853 the first school of photography was established at 309 Regent Street, complete with class rooms, a new glass house studio, and a ladies apartment.

When Quintin Hogg took over in 1882 he set up evening classes in photography, and by the turn of the century the Poly could proudly claim to have the

"first and uniformly most successful
school of photography in the world"

180 years of professional portrait photography

2021 marked a significant anniversary at 309 Regent Street, and to celebrate the 180th birthday of portrait photography, we set up a competition for our students, to enable them to share the thrill and wonder experienced by the Pioneers of Portrait Photography.

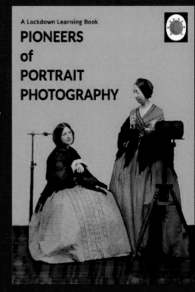

As we were still working under the restrictions of the lockdown, students were sent a goodybag, containing photographic paper, a red plastic "safe light" filter, and a book of instructions, so that they could build and operate their very own steam-punk Victorian Camera, using upcycled materials.

Their portraits were exhibited in the foyer of 309 Regent Street, as part of our celebration event.

It's fun, and it's easy.
We have included the details here, so that you too can have a go!

Modern digital camera for sale
(some assembly required)

" Any sufficiently advanced technology is indistinguishable from magic"
Arthur C. Clarke's third law

In the early days, successful photography was the result of an uneasy alliance between art, luck and science; the unpredictability of the outcome adding to the sense of wonder and excitement.

The simple projects outlined here offer you an opportunity to experience some of the thrill that must have attended those pioneering experimenters, who were exploring a curious new phenomenon, originally known as "photogenic drawing".

By hand-crafting your own photographic portrait in this way we are reminded that the best image making is usually the result of great care and preparation. Attention should be given to the choice of location, skilful composition of the scene, the posture and expression of your sitter, the quality and intensity of the light, and, above all else, selecting just the right moment to click the shutter and thereby commit a fleeting instant to posterity.

Modern digital technology attempts to negate this, encouraging us to side-step all of these nuanced considerations, and fire off endless shots in the vain hope that one of them might be a success. Let's try something a little different.

By reinventing these Victorian marvels as simple kitchen-table projects, we can gain a renewed appreciation for the skill and ingenuity of those amazing pioneers of portrait photography.

This is the earliest known photograph of a photographer at work.

It was taken in Beard's studio in about 1843. The photographer is Jacob Hogg.
If you look closely you will see that Jacob is holding the lens cap, and using his pocket watch to time the exposure.

Here is a digital single-lens reflex camera.
One of the cool things about it is that you can swap the lenses around.

I've gone on holiday, and upon opening my suitcase, I realise that I've left the lens at home!

What can I do?

Let's cover up the front of the camera with kitchen foil, so that no light can get in.

With a needle, we make a tiny hole in the middle of the foil.

What happens if we now try to take a photo with this bizarre contraption..?

We have made a pin hole camera!

The image is blurry - this is because the pin hole was a bit big,
...but not bad for a piece of kitchen foil!

Make a Pinhole Camera

Get a small Pringles tube

Make a pinhole in the middle of the metal base.
Make the hole as small as you can.

cover the hole with black tape

The tape acts as our shutter

Roll up some black paper and insert it into the tube.

This is because most food tubes have a silver lining, and most cameras do not.

Use lots of black tape to cover the plastic lid. You need to use plenty because daylight must not be able to get inside.

... and, er ... that's it !

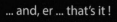

Make a Dark Room

A good darkroom is vital to the success of this project.

This is what your darkroom should look like.

A bathroom makes a great darkroom. Just black out the windows with kitchen foil.

Make a Safe Light

We are using black and white photo paper. It is designed to be slightly less sensitive to red light, so that we can use a weak red light, to see what we are doing.

to make a safe light, cover a torch with red plastic.

You could use the red wrappers from Quality Street sweets.
After extensive research, I believe that *"strawberry delight"* wrappers are the appropriate ones for photographic use.

Load the camera

In the darkroom:

turn on your red safe light

take a piece of photo paper, and cover it with the pringles tube
draw around the tube, using a permanent pen

cut inside the line, to make a circle of photo paper

note:
The black & white photo paper can be purchased online:

We used Kentmere VC select RC
Glossy Photo Paper, (5 x 7 inches)
--about £9 for a pack of 25 sheets.

use a loop of black tape to stick the photo paper to the inside of the lid, with the shiny side of the paper facing outwards.

Put the lid back on the tube.

You can watch a demo video of this process.

Just visit our youtube channel:
"Professor Pepper's Optical Extravaganza"

Go outside: this works best on a sunny day
Find something solid to rest your camera on, and then hold
it down to stop it wobbling.

Point the camera at your subject.
(get in quite close)

Ask them to hold **very still**.
Peel off the tape (your shutter) to reveal the pinhole
Count to 40
Put the tape back on again.

You have just taken your first Victorian photographic portrait!

Lets mix some chemicals and develop it.

Mix the Chemicals

Our processing chemicals can all be bought from the supermarket.

They are (relatively) safe, but try to keep them off your skin.

The developer is a mixture of washing soda, vitamic C tablets, and coffee powder.

measure 200 ml of cold tap water

add 2 teaspoons of washing soda

stir for a minute

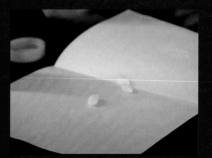

put 3 Vitamin C tablets onto a sheet of paper. (use cheap vitamin C, but not the fizzy ones)

fold over the paper

crush the tablets with a glass bottle, or a rolling pin.

pour this powder into a glass containing 50 ml of warm water
(this is about 5 tablespoons of water)

stir for a minute

When you are ready to start processing your photographs:

add the Vitamin C water to the Washing Soda water.

then stir in 4 teaspoons of instant coffee powder (not decaff)

This mixture is our photo developer. It is called "Caffenol-C"

Pour the developer into a microwave meal tray.

We need to make a "stop bath"
This will be used when we want to stop the development of the negative

Cut the top off a 2 litre lemonade bottle

pour in 1.5 litres of water

add a big squirt of lemon juice

Now prepare a salt solution
This will be used to "fix" the image, so it does not fade to black.

Cut the top off a 2 litre lemonade bottle

pour in 1.5 litres of water

add a whole mug full of salt

stir for a minute

Develop your Negative

In the darkroom, arrange your chemicals in this order:

DEV -- STOP -- FIX

Put them on a sheet of newspaper, to catch any splashes

Turn off all the lights, then turn on your safe light.

carefully remove the photo paper from the Pringles Tube

put it into the tray of DEVELOPER. Make sure it is shiny side UP.

gently tip the tray to agitate the developer

check on progress after one minute

it might take up to 6 minutes for the image to slowly appear, but when you can see a "strong" image, transfer the paper to the STOP for 30 seconds

then transfer it to the FIX

It is going to take a few **hours** to fix the negative, so that it does not fog.

TIPS
If the negative is not forming after 5 minutes try gently warming the DEV by resting it in a larger tray of warm water, for a minute.

If you put your chemicals in a box, you can cover it with a towel when fixing, so that you can then use your bathroom as nature intended.

Make a Positive

After a few hours, wash off the salt solution, using tap water, and a drop of washing up liquid.

... and hang your negative up to dry.

Avoid bright lights - these negatives are a bit fragile.

you can make a positive print in a number of different ways:

1: There are apps which will allow you to reverse a negative on your phone.
This one is free, and is called "Photo Negative Scanner"

or

2: you can scan your negative into a computer, then use the "invert" feature in a paint programme.

In MS Paint: right-click the image, then select "Invert Colors"
In Photoshop: click Image - Invert

or

3: You can go "old school" and make a contact print, which is a print of your print.

Victorian VR

3D Photography is nothing new. It was something of a Victorian craze, and by 1862 there were more stereo prints in production than ordinary 2D ones.

We can build a stereo pinhole camera, using a small cardboard box.

All you need to do is make 2 pinholes, about 5 cm apart.
Try to keep them the same size, because we will be taking 2 photographs which are very nearly identical, apart from the 5 cm shift in orientation.

Put a card divider down the middle of the box, to stop the 2 images from overlapping.

inside the top section of a 3D camera, showing the divider and the two pinholes

note: the base of the box slides into this top section, to make a lightproof seal

"The principle of the stereoscope is copied from nature: i.e., when both eyes are employed in the examination of an object, two similar pictures, embracing dissimiliar forms, are impressed upon the retinae, and produce the effect of solidity. Stereoscopic pictures are obtained by exposing sensitized films in the camera to the picture of an object taken in two positions."

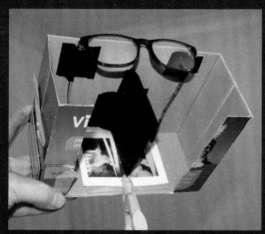

A stereoscope viewer, using pound-shop reading glasses

A stereo pair, taken with the pinhole 3D camera

Adding a lens - the game changer

The problem with a pinhole is... that it's so darn *small*!

The pinhole does not let a lot of light through, so it takes a long time to create an exposure. But if you make the hole bigger, the image gets blurry.
So how can we let more light into the camera, and still create a sharp image?

Professor Pepper knew the secret:

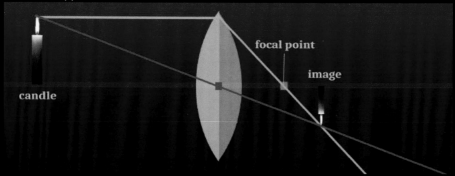

"Convex lenses cause the different rays which pass through them from any given point or object, to bend and unite together again at another point beyond them.
The more convex the lens is, the nearer is its focus."

This was an experiment to really push at the limits of optical "steam punk" photography

This camera is just a cardboard box, with a really big magnifying glass stuck on the front. It's designed to produce the brightest possible image, and was used to create what is probably the first photograph taken with blueprint paper as the film.
Blueprint, or Cyanotype paper can be developed with ordinary tap water. Before the invention of the photocopier, it was often used to copy plans and documents, hence the name.

here is the result:

the negative
*on blueprint paper
after a 7 hour exposure*

the positive
...it's a car!

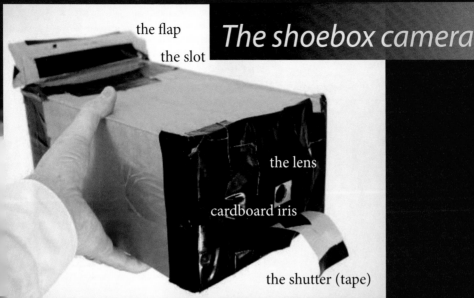

the flap

the slot

the lens

cardboard iris

the shutter (tape)

This camera is made from a shoebox, and a magnifying glass

It is simple to make, and you can see examples of our shoebox photos at the end of this book.

Use black tape to stick the lid down - it needs to be light-proof

Cut a round hole in the front of the shoe box, (about 5 cm in diameter) then tape a magnifying lens over it.

Now cut a slot in the back, so that you can load photo paper, and cover it with a re-sealable flap of black tape.

You cannot adjust the focus of this camera, so we need to work out how far away your subject should be. If you look through the flap, you should be able to see an image on the back wall inside the box.

Walk carefully towards a bright window or a table lamp, until its image is in focus. Add a piece of string to the front of the box, measuring the distance from your camera to the window or lamp.

Now we have found the focussing distance, we need to reduce the "iris". Cover the lens with card, leaving an 8mm diameter hole in the middle. Reducing the size of the iris will improve the picture quality considerably.

Finally, add a strip of tape to act as the shutter.

To take a photo, load some paper in the darkroom, go outside, prop up the box, get someone to stand so the end of the string touches their nose, and try an exposure time of about 5 seconds.

using string to focus

shoebox camera negative

a 2 second exposure in direct sunlight. 6 minutes processing time in Caffenol-C
Fixed overnight in a salt solution. Negative is shown actual size.
The brown tint is caused by the coffee

a positive print

The negative was scanned, opened in Photoshop, flipped horizontally, and inverted.
Printed onto glossy paper with an inkjet printer

The Amazing Lumiere Brothers

Louis and Auguste Lumiere have been credited with the invention of cinema; screening a demonstration of their Cinematographe machine in a Paris Cafe in December 1895, and a few weeks later bringing motion pictures to Britain, when they presented their films at the Poly's theatre, thereby gifting us with the world's first cinema.

2021 brought the 125th anniversary of this historic landmark, and we set up a number of student projects to celebrate.

Photo-Grass

We set out to make a gigantic portrait of the Lumiere brothers, on the lawn outside our Harrow Campus Halls of Residency.

This was to be a photograph, some 2,750 square meters in size, where the photo-sensitive material is grass.

Using sheets of black plastic we created a "negative" image of the portrait on the field, and allowed the grass to fade beneath. When we removed the negative, a positive image was left on the lawn.

Connor Turansky from the Emerging Media Space flew our drone above it, to get a good look at the results.

The story was subsequently showcased on the BBC News website.

Kerrie Portman, Animation BA Honours student, said:

"I loved this project because honouring the Lumiere Brothers, the pioneers of cinema, by masking their photo onto the grass is so unique!
Film-making and digital entertainment is now done predominantly with technology, so it's nice to celebrate their anniversary by integrating the organic life-cycle of grass"

Photo: Connor Turansky

The Race for Cinema

When struggling French photographer Antoine Lumiere was drafted into the army, he left his two sons in charge of his photographic film factory, which was on the brink of bankruptcy.

By the time he returned, the brothers had created an automated production line, and hired a staff of 12 people.

These brothers were Auguste and Louis Lumiere.
Auguste was 20, and Louis 18.

Antoine (centre) and his sons,
Auguste (L) and Louis (R)

Over in the USA, Thomas Edison had joined a fiercely competitive race to develop motion picture technology.

Being Edison, his camera ran on mains electricity, and the film was not projected, but displayed inside a cabinet, so that only one person at a time could watch it through a peep hole.
Edison did not think that film projection was financially viable.

In 1895 Antoine Lumiere attended a demonstration of Edison's Kinetoscope film viewer.
He brought home a sample of the movie film and instructed his sons to find a way to project it.

The brothers set to work, and corrected many of the technical flaws that they perceived in the rival technology.

the film was 35mm wide, and set the standard for movies

Their machine was called the Cinematographe, and unlike Edison's camera, it was hand cranked. Weighing only 7kg, it could be taken out on location, and almost all of their films were shot out doors.

What's more, the Cinematographe could also be used as a film printer, making positive copies from the original negatives, and could then act as a projector.

At the heart of their amazing device was a claw mechanism based on a sewing machine.

This technology was so successful that it was then adopted by all other camera makers, and set the standard for the next 100 years.

On 22nd March 1895, the brothers successfully projected a film onto a screen using their prototype cinematographe.

At this screening, Louis met an engineer called Jules Carpentier, who offered to help refine the design, and then mass produce the machine.

The Lumieres were based in the town of Lyon, and Carpentier's workshop was in Paris, which is over 300 miles away. They could only collaborate by post, and it was crucial that everything should be ready for December 28th 1895, the date booked for the first public performance at the Salon Indien of the Grand Café.

Firm commitments had been made, and there was not a moment to lose as many other rival inventors were racing to be the first to perfect the technology and thereby dominate the market.

It was their dad, Antoine, who insisted on the rushed premiere in the Paris Cafe, and he organised the event.

It seems to have been a bit of a shambles.

For a start, he forgot to invite Jules Carpentier, who was heartbroken to have missed this historic milestone.

Needless to say, the Parisian entertainment industry was blown away by this innovation: the Folies Bergers offered the equivalent of £200,000 for a cinematographe machine, but dad said "*non*!"

A stage magician called Georges Melies was a family friend. He offered 10 thousand gold French Francs for a machine, but Antoine also turned him down, saying;

*" Don't waste your money, Georges.
It's just a passing fad, with no future!"*

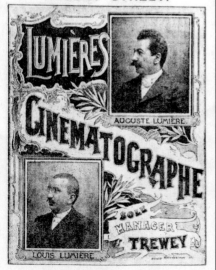

On 21st February 1896, 2 months after the Paris show, the Lumiere Cinematographe was demonstrated here at the Polytechnic to a paying audience, establishing it as the birthplace of British cinema.

As far as we can tell, it was at this screening that they premiered what became the first iconic moment of cinema; when a train arrives at a station. Apparently the audience were so alarmed that some of them ran screaming from the hall!

Lumiere 125 logo

We ran a competition to design a logo for all of the projects that were taking place under the Lumiere 125 Scheme.
The winning logo was created by Ilirian Camaj, a level 4 animation student.

Ilirian Camaj

Felicity Neal

Akua Brooks

Bozhidar Gospodinov

George Sheard

Nadine Abdelaziz

Roni Laszczyk

The Lumies

The Lumie Awards were presented to our winning film-makers.

The Lumiere Train is depicted in 3D, running on tracks of movie film to usher in the age of cinema

WORLD RECORD HOLDER

The Longest Wait for a Film Sequel: 125 years, 7 months and 5 days

21 February 1896 – 26 September 2021

Both screenings occurring at REGENT STREET CINEMA UNIVERSITY OF WESTMINSTER

Lumiere 125 logo designed by Ilirian Camaj and modelled in 3D by Simon Gape

We ran a film-making competition, open to all University of Westminster students.
The challenge was to shoot a sequel to one of the Lumiere Brothers' films.
We screened the winning movies at the cinema, establishing a very unusual
world record!

"Victorians" 1896
by Louis Lumiere

"Elizabethans" 2021
by Vanja Ivkovic

"Paris Rush Hour" 1896
by Louis Lumiere

"London Rush Hour" 2021
by Arundathi Ekanayake

"Boules" 1896
by Louis Lumiere

"Tennis" 2021
by Mina Angeletti

"Soldiers" 1896
by Louis Lumiere

"Soldiers" 2021
by Allistair McDowall

...and another thing...

As you will recall, Georges Melies was not permitted to buy a *Cinematographe*, so on the same day that the Lumieres screened their first films here at Regent Street, Georges popped over to the Finsbury Park Technical College, to see a demonstration of a British movie system called the *Theatrograph*.

... and yes reader, he bought one! Apparently it was *dreadful*.

Georges called his temperamental new camera *"the coffee grinder"*, as it constantly jammed. It was when releasing one such jam that he accidentally invented his first film effect – a jump cut, where a carriage appears to turn into a hearse.

This effectively kick-started his career as a cine-magician, and he went on to produce many fantastical masterpieces.

It is interesting to reflect that had it not been for inferior British film technology, the special effects industry might never have happened!

An Autochrome photograph of Louis' daughter, Andree

A modern RGB display (*detail*)

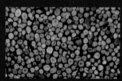

A Lumiere Autochrome filter (*detail*)

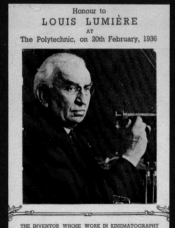

Honour to
LOUIS LUMIÈRE
AT
The Polytechnic, on 20th February, 1936

THE INVENTOR WHOSE WORK IN KINEMATOGRAPHY
PROVIDED THE FIRST SHOW OF MOVING PICTURES
TO THE PAYING PUBLIC FORTY YEARS AGO AT

THE POLYTECHNIC
20th FEBRUARY, 1896

The Lumiere brothers were also responsible for other innovations:

In 1903 they launched the autochrome colour photography system. Amazingly, they had found a way to make colour photographs using black and white film.

Their solution is remarkably similar to modern screen technology, but instead of pixels, the brothers used coloured grains of potato starch to build up their vividly coloured slides.

By the 1930s Louis was making movies in 3D, and in 1936 the Polytechnic invited him back to Regent Street to celebrate the 40th anniversary of cinema.

Auguste Lumiere was a medical pioneer, and he produced the very first X-Ray photograph of a broken bone. X-rays are a form of radiation, which can be "seen" on film.

To celebrate this achievement, I attempted to make my own X-Ray image, using Brazil Nuts as the source of radiation.

DATA SHEET: BRAZIL NUTS
Radioactivity: 6,600 pCi/kg

Radio Isotopes Present
Radium-226
Potassium-40
Radon-228

Radiation Types Emitted
Beta Particles
Alpha Particles
Gamma Radiation

I sealed a big sheet of black and white photographic film in a thick lightproof bag, loaded it with Brazil nuts, covered it all over with blackout fabric, and left it in my office.

A few weeks later we went into lockdown, and so I was only able to return to collect it some 17 months later.

To be honest, I was not expecting much, but I processed the film anyway:
... and this is what I got:

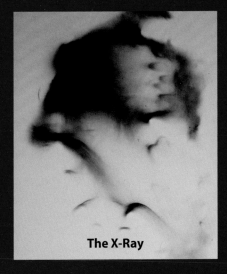

The X-Ray

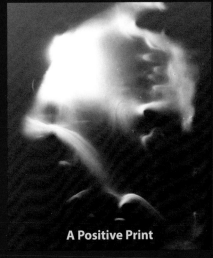

A Positive Print

309 Regent Street

We scheduled our big celebration event for the very first week that we were able to return to University, after the lockdown.

In the marble foyer at 309 Regent Street we exhibited the winners of the Victorian Steampunk Portrait Photography competition.

Denisa Zajacova
BA (Hons) Fine Art Mixed Media
Portrait of Chloe
Developed with Nescafe Gold Blend

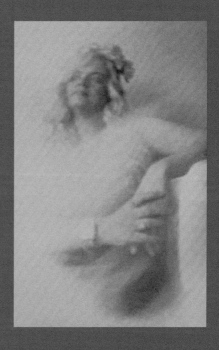

Christy Higgs
BA (Hons) Fashion
Self Portrait
Developed with Alcafe Instant

Gyorgy Englert
BA (Hons) Photography
Bill and Gabriel in their garden,
before Gabriel's 82nd birthday
Developed with Sainsbury's Barista Edition

Kristina Hristova
BA (Hons) Journalism
Portrait of Vanya
Developed with Alcafe Gold Roast

"People on the street
stare at their phones mindlessly as if
life could be eternal.
But only after making a Victorian Camera
are you able to frame a soul on a photo paper."

Damira Pilizota
BA (Hons) Media & Communicaiton Design
Portrait of Marko
Developed with Magico Coffee Powder

Ranita Hameed
MSc (Hons) Project Management
Self Portrait
Developed with Nescafe

Helena Henning
BSc (Hons) Human Nutrition
Trellic Tower
Developed with Hubbard's Foodstore Instant

Fiona Nashie
BSc (Hons) Biomedical Science
Steam Punk Camera

We then went next door, to celebrate the history of our cinema.

We started with a recital of movie themes by Donald MacKenzie, using the cinema's 1936 Compton theatre organ, followed by Julie Marsh's installation art piece, where a laser was guided around the interior of the space, simultaneously accompanied by a point-of-view video screened by the projection equipment.

Arundathi recieves her "Lumie" award from our guest of honour, Michael Rosen.

By screening the 4 winning student films, we established a very quirky world record.

"the longest wait for a film sequel"

During our "Victorian PowerPoint" magic lantern presentation, Stephen Ryley demonstrated how Pepper summoned a Ghost onto this very stage...

... and conjoured giant sea monsters from a tiny drop of Victorian Tap Water

We were keen to recreate these illusions, as Pepper developed a reputation for staging them in our optical theatre.

"... infinitesimal creatures in a drop of Thames water appeared like antediluvian animals engaged in combat..."

Peppers' demonstration obviously had quite an effect, because the shop next door started selling water filters!

The Portrait Studio

To celebrate the 180th anniversary of portrait photography at 309 Regent Street, we set up our own studio. In keeping with the Victorian steam punk ethos, we used shoebox cameras to take the photos.

The glass pyramid which once lit the original studio has long since been removed, so we improvised using a giant concave mirror to focus September sunlight from Regent Street onto our subjects. Even then, the exposure time was 10 seconds per shot.

A team of animation students ran the studio, and Simon our unflappable technician organised the processing lab, where the negatives were developed using instant coffee and washing soda.
Guests were photographed during the private view of the exhibition, and the portraits were collected as they left the cinema.

PIONEERS
of PORTRAIT PHOTOGRAPHY

Portrait Photography Returns to Regent Street

On Sunday 26th September 2021 we celebrated the 180th anniversary of Europe's first commercial portrait studio, by bringing portrait photography back to 309 Regent Street.

The portraits were taken with our steam-punk camera, which uses a magnifying glass as a lens.

The photographs were processed with Tesco's coffee powder.

We posted the portraits as the afternoon went on...

Birthplace of Commercial Portrait Photography

Europe's first Commercial Portrait Photography Studio
was opened in this building on 23rd March 1841.

Birthplace of British Cinema

In this cinema, the Lumière Cinématographe
premiered to the press on 20th February 1896
and the next day gave the first cinema show
to a paying audience in Britain.

Michael Rosen unveiled a commemorative plaque in the foyer of 309 Regent Street.

Reflecting on the celebration, Michael Rosen said:
"The event at the University of Westminster was uplifting, inspiring, hugely informative and great fun too! It was fascinating to hear how we were commemorating a key moment in the history of cinema... I hope that I will be able to keep up some kind of connection with the film, animation and photography department in the future."

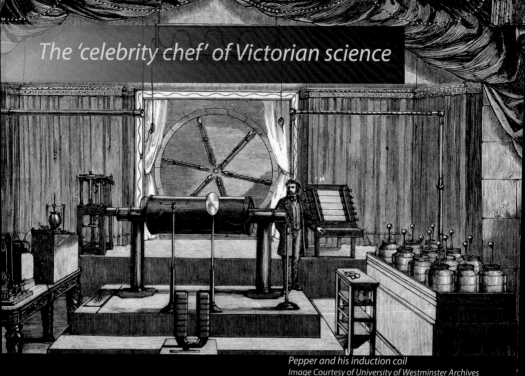

Pepper and his induction coil
Image Courtesy of University of Westminster Archives

I think you would have liked John Henry Pepper.

His comprehensive understanding of scientific principles was brilliantly complemented by his charismatic showmanship.

Pepper made the emerging worlds of science and new technology accessible to the general public through lightning-fast demonstrations. Like a modern-day close-up magician, the professor performed one scientific marvel after another, leaving his audience gasping with astonishment. In hundreds of demonstrations he traversed all of the phenomena of physical nature; mechanics, pneumatics, optics, heat, electricity, magnetism, chemistry and astronomy.

Some experiments involved simple items that you could find around the house, others required special equipment and expensive materials. He once incinerated an equal weight of coal, and diamond, to demonstrate that they were both forms of carbon.

In another, he filled a jar to the brim with alcohol, and then managed to stuff the jar with a large quantity of cotton wool, without any alcohol overflowing.
This startling illustration was followed by a series of investigations to demonstrate that matter is made of atoms.

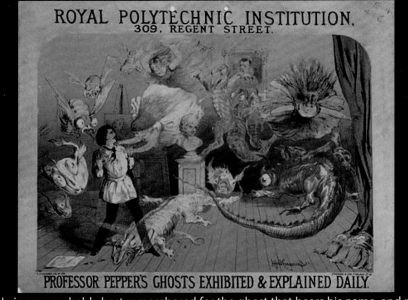

He is now probably best remembered for the ghost that bears his name, and not only did he exhibit this stage illusion, but he also revealed its secrets.

It is perhaps a consequence of this scientifically rational approach to the macabre that led him to dedicate his attention to debunking spiritualists, exposing the trickery behind deceptive magic by demonstrating his own staged versions of their effects, such as the levitation of tables, and the production of "ectoplasm".

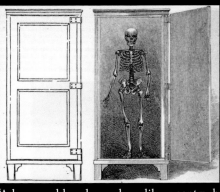

Pepper invented another illusion which has continued to amaze us.

He called it the "Proteus Cabinet".
Let's hear the Professor explain it in his own words:

"A large and handsome box, like a sentry-box on wheels, and raised from the floor so that the spectators could see under, over, and all round it, is wheeled onto the platform. On being opened it appeared to be well lighted from the top by an ordinary railway carriage lamp, and seemed perfectly empty.

The assistant now being invited to enter the box, the door is closed and locked, and, after a few minutes have elapsed, is re-opened, when a skeleton appeared to be standing in the very place where the living being had been formerly observed.

Again the door is closed, and the next time it is opened, the skeleton has vanished, and the assistant walks out of the box with a carpet bag."

Pepper published a number of important texts which further helped to popularise science. These include his "*Boys Playbook of Science*", which became the key school science text book in the USA for decades.

He followed this with "*Scientific Amusements for Young People*" and "*Cyclopaedic Science simplified*", all with the common aim of helping the next generation thrive in the emerging new world of technology and innnovation. In the "*Playbook of Metals*" we find that Pepper is way ahead of his time, contemplating the possibility of continental drift.

His books are generously illustrated throughout, with etchings based on his own drawings, helping to convey something of the vivid immediacy of his lectures.

All of the Professor's quotes used this book have been taken from his writings, and I have also included some of his extraordinary illustrations.

FIG. 95.—*Exhibition of the Photodrome at the Polytechnic.*

Pepper left the Polytechnic and embarked on a lecture tour of the English-speaking world, and a global audience marvelled at his abilty to conduct one experiment after another in quick and almost magical succession.

It was whilst touring Australia (and about 5 years before Conan Doyle started penning his Sherlock Holmes stories) that Pepper was engaged by the Brisbane Police Force as a consulting chemist, having published a paper on methods to detect strychnine poisoning.

ANNOUNCEMENT EXTRAORDINARY.

THE GREAT SCIENTIFIC EXPERI-MENT OF
TAPPING THE CLOUDS !
OR,
RAIN-MAKING !
Will be attempted on the
BRISBANE RACECOURSE,
ON SATURDAY NEXT, 4TH FEBRUARY,
BY PROFESSOR J. H. PEPPER.
To prevent overcrowding in the vicinity of the Professor's Apparatus, a small nominal charge of SIXPENCE admission to the Course will be made.
All applications for Lease of Booths, Stalls, and Sites, &c., to be addressed to Secretary of Q. T. Club, Queen-street, immediately.
SPECIAL OMNIBUSES AND STEAMERS. 1292

He also seems to have taken an interest in environmental matters, because when Queensland suffered an intense and prolonged heat wave, leading to a serious drought, he devised a rainmaking experiment.

Pepper managed to collect a range of highly volatile materials, including a fleet of rockets from HMS Cormorant, a land mine, ten swivel guns, and many barrels of gunpowder.
Things did not go entirely to plan: Pepper could not launch his "cloud compelling" kites, one of his guns exploded, and a rocket flew off horizontally, narrowly missing the crowds who had gathered to watch the spectacle.

... and it did not rain.

Thank You

This work was a team effort, and mostly took place during the restrictions of lockdown. I am very grateful to the students, who have shown such positivity, resilience and good humour thoughout.
There are many others who have been instrumental in the success of this enterprise.
I apologies if I have inadvertantly missed anyone out:

My fellow course leaders, for promoting the projects to their locked-down students,
Anna McNally, our senior archivist, who sourced the brilliant images of 309 Regent Street
Professor Jonathan Stockdale, for allowing us to mess up his lawn
Dr. Sal Jarvis, the champion of our Lumiere 125 scheme
The staff at the Regent Street Cinema
Steve McCombe, Connor Turanksy and Simon Gape, our remarkable technical whizzkids
Our Head of School, Michaela O'Brien, for her relentless support
Professor Janet Jones, head of DCDI
Our Vice Chancellor Dr. Peter Bonfield, for his frequent words of encouragement,
Henry Fraser and the team at Windfall Films
Dave Freeman and Simon Westgate in the Photography department
Usha Dahyabhai, for sorting out the endless purchase orders
Claire Linge at the Heath Robinson Museum

...and, of course, Michael Rosen, for becoming our honorary Professor Pepper.

Steampunk Shopping List

If you want to try your hand at Victorian Photography, here is a list of the kit we used.

a torch
black marker pen
black tape
kitchen timer
shoebox
pringles tube (40g)
pin
kitchen foil
black card
magnifying glass (£1 from Wilko)
string
3 lemonade bottles
microwave meal tray
red plastic of some kind for the safelight

Hopefully you will have most of this already:

Now pop to the supermarket to buy the chemicals:

Washing Soda Crystals
Instant Coffee (not decaff)
Vitamin C tablets (not the fizzy ones)
Lemon Juice
Table Salt

The black & white photo paper can be purchased online:

We used Kentmere VC select RC Glossy Photo Paper, (5 x 7 inches) --about £9 for a pack of 25 sheets.